RACING CARS

Design	David West
	Children's Book Design
Designer	Keith Newell
Editor	Yvonne Ibazebo
Picture Researcher	Emma Krikler
Illustrators	Simon Tegg and David Burroughs

© Aladdin Books Ltd 1992

First published in
the United States in 1992 by
Gloucester Press
95 Madison Avenue
New York, NY 10016

Library of Congress
Cataloging-in-Publication Data

de Vere, Charles.
  Racing cars / by Charles de Vere
    p. cm. — (Let's look up)
  Includes index.
  Summary: Traces the development of the
racing car, discusses Grand Prix winners as well
as other types of racers, and provides
information on famous drivers and racing
circuits.
  ISBN 0-531-17380-1
  1. Grand Prix racing—Juvenile literature.
2. Automobile racing drivers—Juvenile literature.
3. Automobiles, Racing—History—Juvenile
literature. [Automobiles, Racing. 2. Automobile
racing. 3. Grand Prix racing.] I. Series.
GV1029.R554 1992
796.7'2—dc20   92-9551 CIP AC

Printed in Belgium   93-739

LET'S LOOK UP

RACING CARS

CHARLES DE VERE

GLOUCESTER PRESS
New York · London · Toronto · Sydney

Contents

About this book

You can decide for yourself how to read this book. You can simply read it straight through, or you can follow the arrows to find out more about a subject before you go on. The choice is yours!

Follow the arrows if you want to know more...

Introduction

The first car races took place in France during the 1890s. But only a few wealthy people could afford to take part, and the cars were quite unreliable and slow. Today's racing cars can travel at speeds of over 200 miles an hour. The sport is also much safer now, and drivers wear various equipment for protection, such as helmets and fireproof clothing.

Racing cars have developed into very fast machines that can travel at great speeds.

The racing car

There are various types of racing cars, but the best known are the single-seat racing cars that take part in the Grand Prix. These racing cars are divided into "formulas," and each formula has a set engine size, car size, and weight. Modern cars have a distinctive shape, with wings at the back and front and a streamlined shape. The wings help to keep the car on the track when it travels at high speeds.

The front, back, and side view of a racing car shows its distinctive shape.

How are racing cars designed?

Today's racing cars are designed using a computer. The system is known as Computer Aided Design (CAD). The old method, which was much slower, involved building a model for testing.

How do computers help car engines perform better? → PAGE 14

Parts of a racing car

A race car is a very complicated vehicle.
Every part, from the engine and suspension to
the tires and brakes, is designed to make the
car fast and safe. Because race cars travel at
such high speeds, their bodies are
streamlined to help them move through the
air easily. Race cars
also lie closer to
the ground to
prevent air from
getting under
them and tipping
them over.

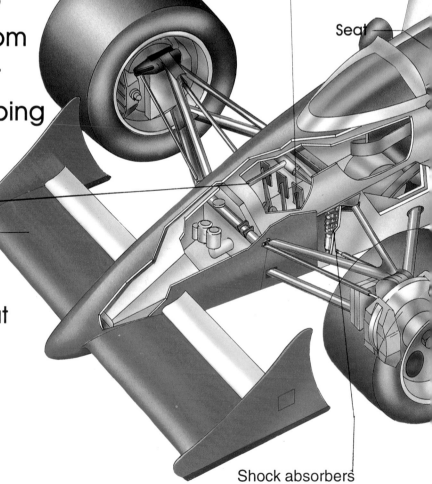

Pedals

Seat

Steering column

Front wing

Shock absorbers

Race cars have
many features that
help them move
smoothly along
the ground, such
as a flat shape,
wings, and wide
tires.

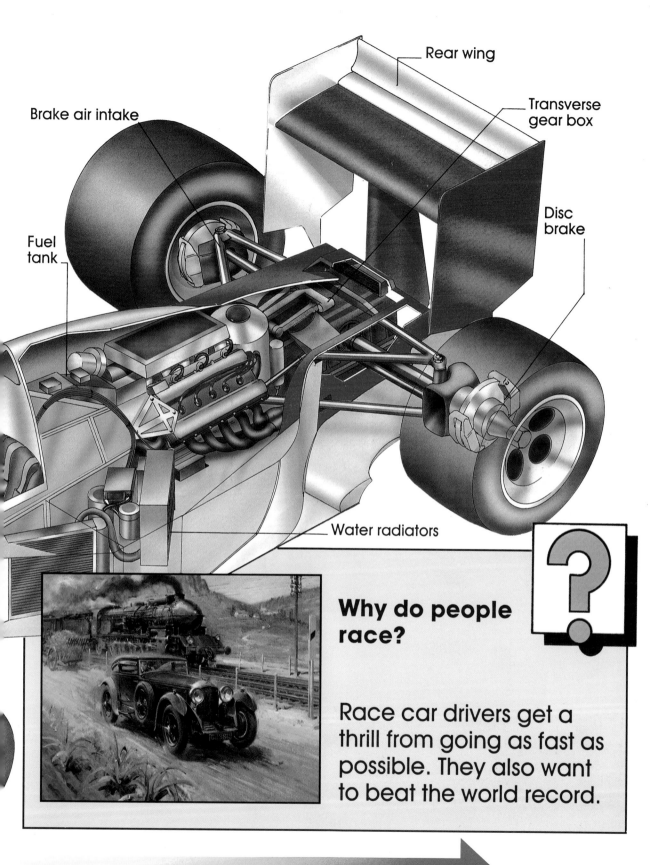

Rear wing

Transverse gear box

Brake air intake

Disc brake

Fuel tank

Water radiators

Why do people race?

Race car drivers get a thrill from going as fast as possible. They also want to beat the world record.

To find out how other racing cars look, turn to Types of racing cars

PAGE 26

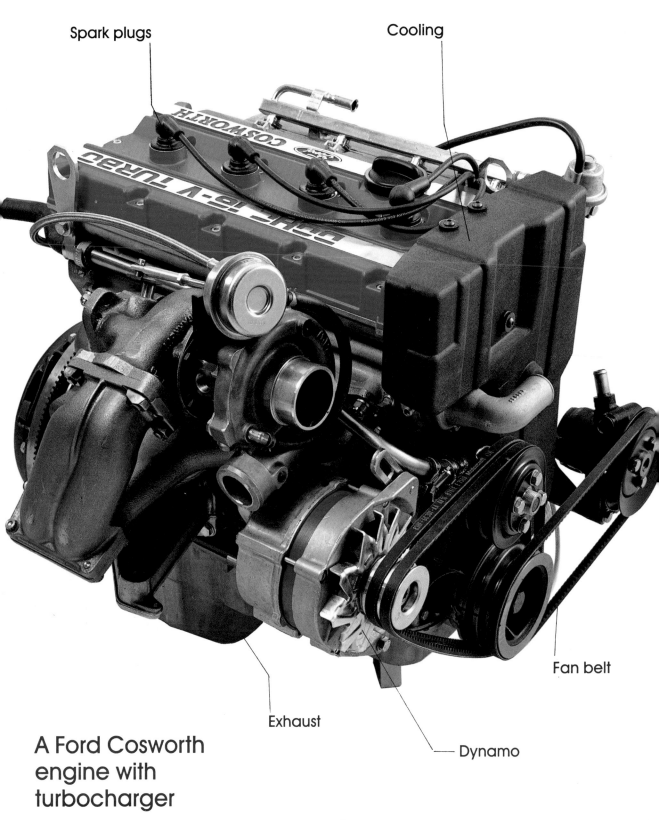

Spark plugs

Cooling

Fan belt

Exhaust

Dynamo

A Ford Cosworth
engine with
turbocharger

The engine

The engine of a race car works in the same way as that of a family car. A carburetor mixes the gasoline with air before passing it onto the engine's cylinders. A spark explodes the mixture, forming hot gases which push the pistons down. A crankshaft changes the up-and-down movement into a rotary motion, which drives the gearbox and the wheels.

What is the transmission for?

The transmission allows the engine to drive the car slowly when starting the car, and faster at higher speeds.

If you want to know more about racing car engines, turn to Types of engines

PAGE 30

More power

Some race car engines use a turbocharger to make them more powerful. The turbo, as it is called, is powered by hot exhaust gases from the engine. It consists of a turbine with blades that are spun at high speed by the exhaust gases. The turbine works a fan which compresses air, and increases the pressure of the air-fuel mix entering the engine. This gives greater engine power.

See which other cars use turbochargers. **PAGE 24**

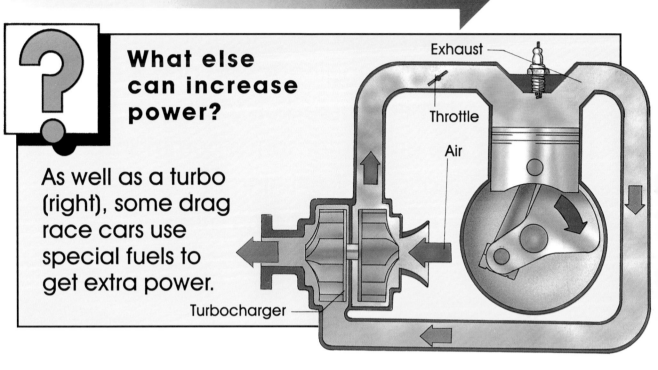

What else can increase power?

As well as a turbo (right), some drag race cars use special fuels to get extra power.

Exhaust

Throttle

Air

Turbocharger

The side view of two racing cars from a clip of Tom Cruise's movie, Days of Thunder.

Computer control

Modern racing cars use computers to ensure that engines give the best performance. Sensors detect the engine speed and the information is then passed on to the computer. The computer sends commands to the engine that alter the timing of the spark plugs, giving maximum engine efficiency.

A race driver may have a computer screen to give him data about the engine.

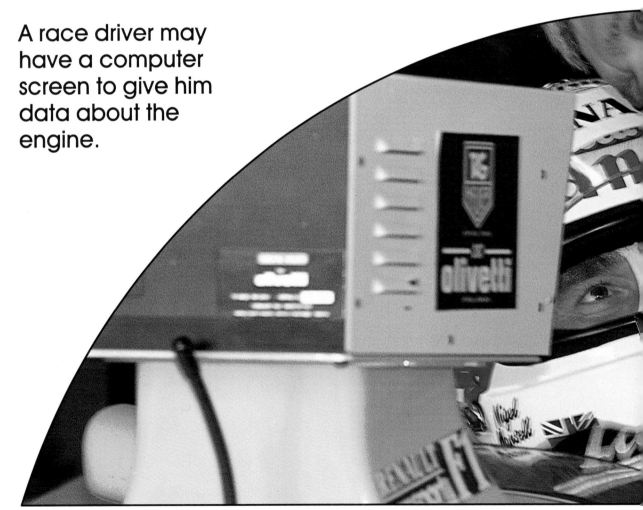

If you want to know more about racing car engines, turn to Types of engines

PAGE 30

Where is the computer?

The onboard computer is usually tucked in front of the engine. It may be able to radio data to the pits during a race.

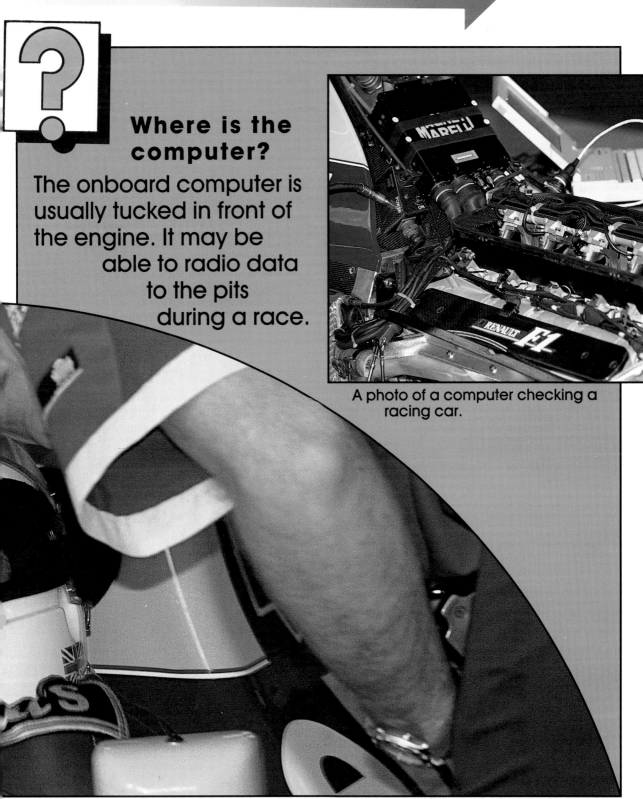

A photo of a computer checking a racing car.

Gripping the road

The power from the engine of a racing car is wasted if it cannot be applied to the road. So tires grip the road and help the car move very fast without skidding. It may seem strange that the best tires for a dry road are smooth – they are called slicks. Only in wet weather do drivers need tires with a good tread pattern – they are called rain tires.

How does suspension help?

With ordinary suspension, the outer wheels of a car tend to lift at a bend.

Active suspension pushes the outer wheels down onto the track.

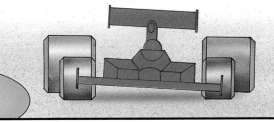

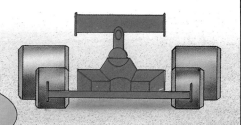

If you want to know what drivers wear during racing, turn to Safety

PAGE 20

The best tires for a dry track are wide, smooth ones, used during Indianapolis races, shown left.

How do drivers shift gear in a Formula 1 car?

Most racing cars use a shift lever, and a clutch to change gear. But the latest cars have gadgets on the steering wheel that change gear automatically.

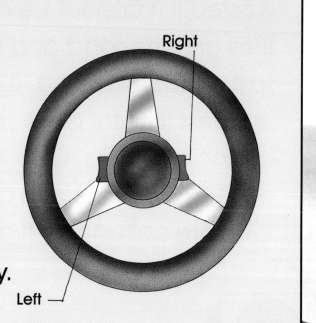

Right

Left

Driving a racing car

Driving a racing car should be similar to driving a family car. But in reality it is very different. The cars go at very high speeds and therefore drivers need to react quickly to any problems. The driver's body also has to withstand the forces caused by rapid acceleration and braking. There are few instruments in the cockpit – the driver has to keep his or her eyes on the road at all times.

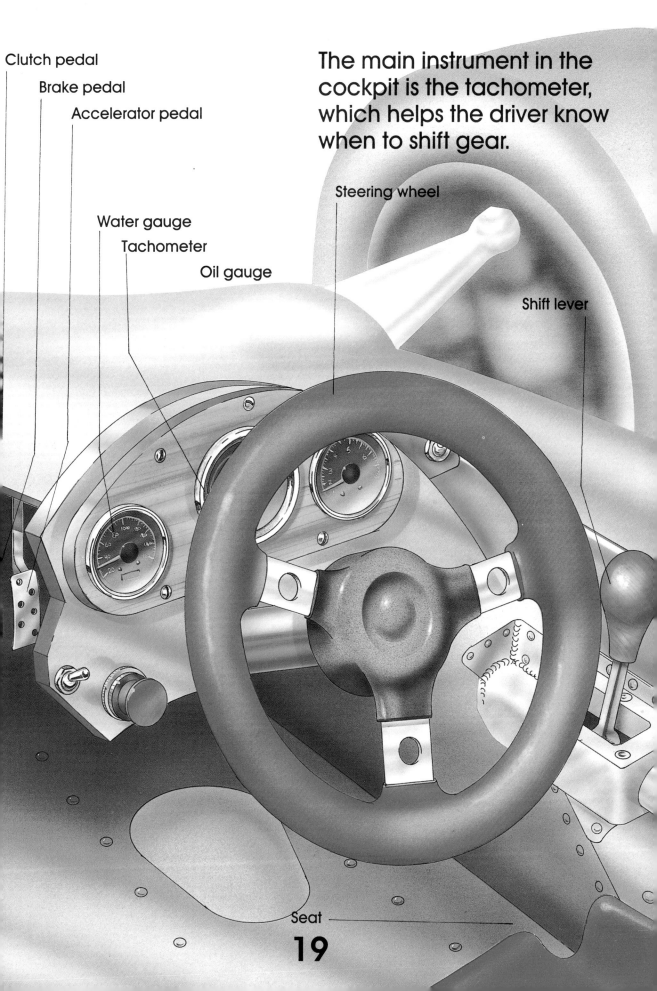

Clutch pedal

Brake pedal

Accelerator pedal

The main instrument in the cockpit is the tachometer, which helps the driver know when to shift gear.

Steering wheel

Water gauge

Tachometer

Oil gauge

Shift lever

Seat

19

Safety

Modern motor racing has been made as safe as possible for drivers and spectators. The cockpit of a modern racing car is surrounded by a strong metal cage. In the event of an accident, the cage holds the driver safely even if the rest of the car falls apart. Built-in fire extinguishers automatically put out small fires, such as those from burning oil, and the driver wears safety clothing.

Drivers can now survive terrible accidents on the race track.

PAGE 28

What does a driver wear for safety?

A safety helmet and fireproof clothing are the driver's main protection. A pipe feeds him oxygen in the event of a fire.

Helmet

Oxygen pipe

Visor

Face mask and fireproof clothing

21

The racing circuit

To cope safely with the high speeds of modern cars, most races are held on specially made tracks, or circuits. Exceptions include the Monaco Grand Prix (which is run through the streets of the town), car rallies, and cross-country events. Marshals use colored flags to warn drivers of possible dangers. On racing circuits, crash barriers prevent cars from going far off the track.

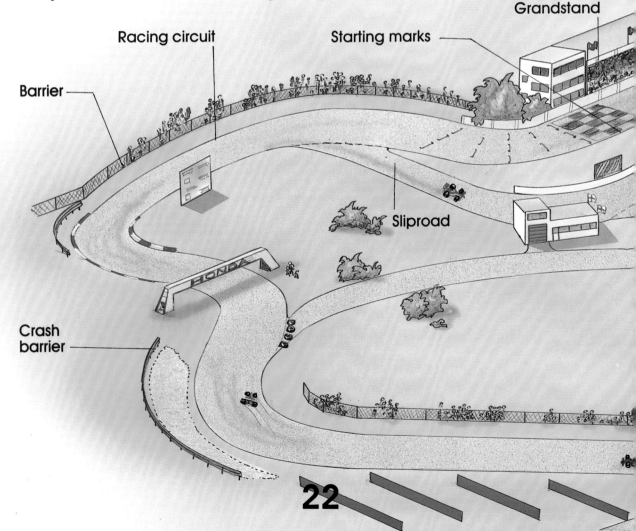

Grandstand

Racing circuit

Starting marks

Barrier

Sliproad

Crash barrier

What happens in the pits?

Cars refuel in the pits. They also change worn tires or put on special ones if the weather changes.

How do drivers know when the race is over? → PAGE 29

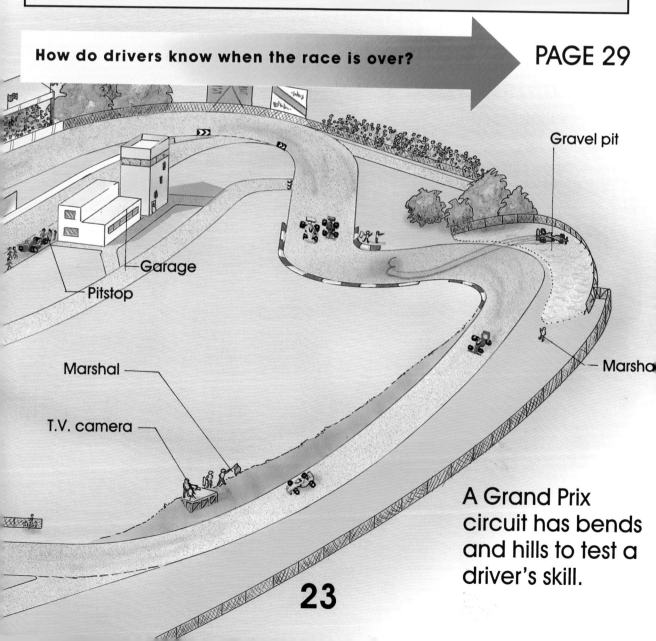

Gravel pit

Garage

Pitstop

Marshal

T.V. camera

Marshal

A Grand Prix circuit has bends and hills to test a driver's skill.

Special racing cars

Among the fastest of all cars are dragsters. Dragsters race in pairs along a straight track for a distance of about one-quarter mile. They can reach speeds of up to 250 miles per hour in less than 6 seconds, and often they use nitromethane fuel instead of gasoline. Funny cars are dragsters with the body based on that of an ordinary car. Other specials include hill climbers and stock cars.

To find out about other types of circuits, turn to Types of racing cars

PAGE 26

How do dragsters slow down?

As well as disc brakes, dragsters use parachutes to slow them down after a one-quarter mile run.

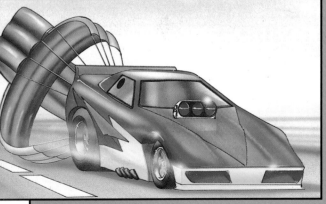

Dragsters are the fastest racing cars. The one in this picture is racing at Santa Pod in England.

Types of cars

Car manufacturers build different types of cars to suit different kinds of racing. This all adds to the variety and excitement for drivers and spectators.

◁ The glamor car of motor sport is the single-seater Formula 1 car.

▷ Cars for the Le Mans 24-hour race are built for endurance.

◁ Saloon car racers are often high-performance production cars.

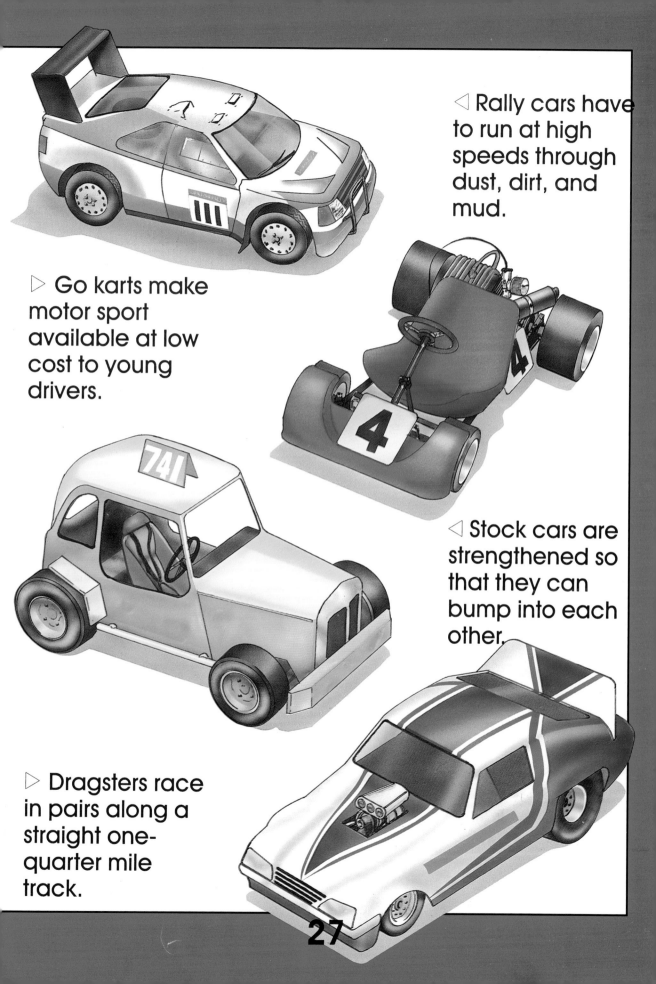

◁ Rally cars have to run at high speeds through dust, dirt, and mud.

▷ Go karts make motor sport available at low cost to young drivers.

◁ Stock cars are strengthened so that they can bump into each other.

▷ Dragsters race in pairs along a straight one-quarter mile track.

The history

Car racing dates back over 100 years. The first races were held on roads in France, but accidents led to the building of special car racing circuits.

The first "car" was a 1769 steam carriage for pulling guns (above).

The 1934 Mercedes W25B (below) reached 176 mph.

The 1924 Miller 183 (left) had a top speed of 156 mph.

The supercharged Bentley of 1930 (right) was built as a road car.

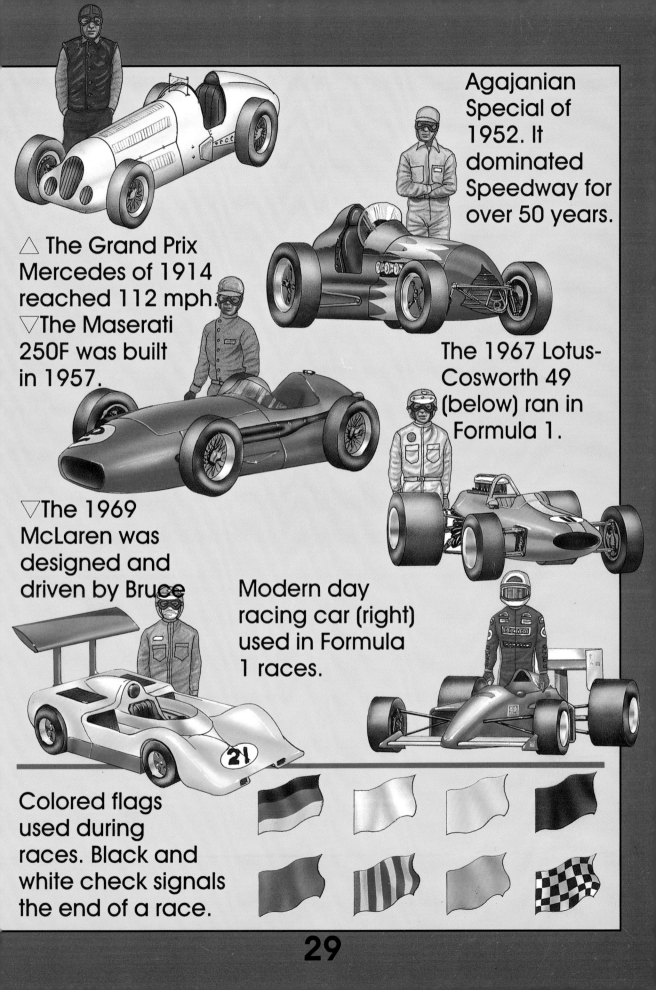

Agajanian Special of 1952. It dominated Speedway for over 50 years.

△ The Grand Prix Mercedes of 1914 reached 112 mph.
▽The Maserati 250F was built in 1957.

The 1967 Lotus-Cosworth 49 (below) ran in Formula 1.

▽The 1969 McLaren was designed and driven by Bruce

Modern day racing car (right) used in Formula 1 races.

Colored flags used during races. Black and white check signals the end of a race.

Types of engines

There are various ways the cylinders are arranged in racing car engines. Some are arranged in line, some in the shape of a V, and some lie flat (see next page). Also, different types of racing cars have the engine in different positions. A mid or rear engine, behind the driver, is common.

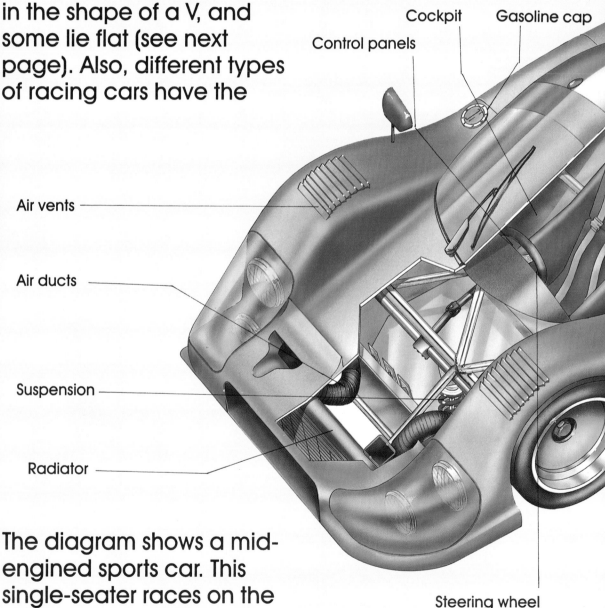

Control panels

Cockpit

Gasoline cap

Air vents

Air ducts

Suspension

Radiator

Steering wheel

The diagram shows a mid-engined sports car. This single-seater races on the track, not on roads.

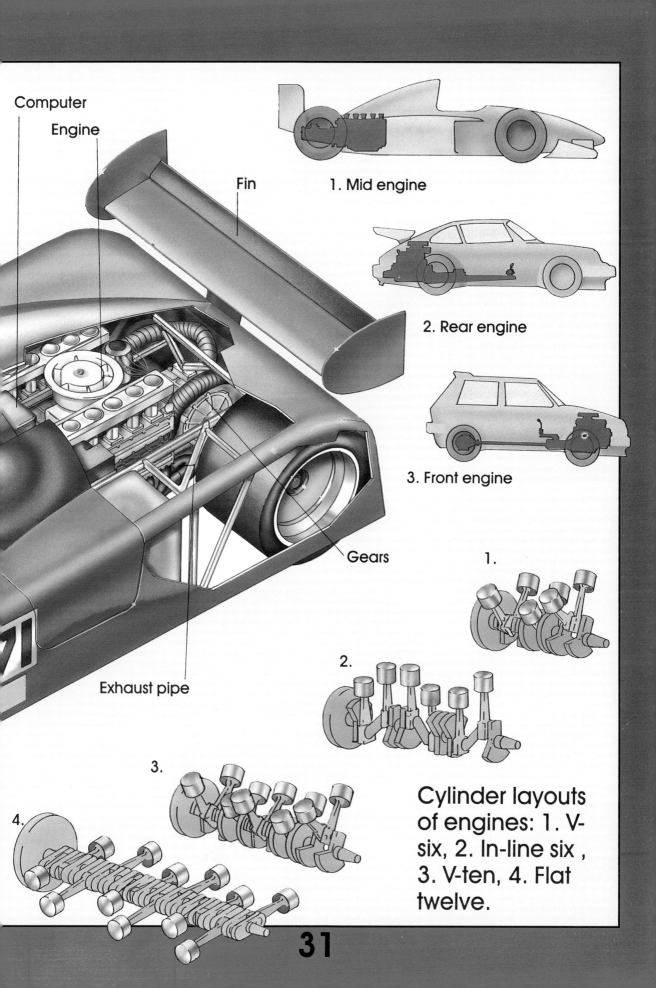

Computer

Engine

Fin

1. Mid engine

2. Rear engine

3. Front engine

Gears

Exhaust pipe

1.

2.

3.

4.

Cylinder layouts of engines: 1. V-six, 2. In-line six , 3. V-ten, 4. Flat twelve.

GLOSSARY

CAD Computer Aided Design. A computer system used to design cars.

Cockpit The area in a racing car where the driver sits.

Disc brake A steel disc attached to the wheels that stops them from moving.

Pits A row of garages along a race track where drivers stop to refuel or change tires.

Spark plug A metal prong which ignites the fuel/air mixture.

Turbocharger A pump that increases the power of a racing car engine.

INDEX

Photocredits
Pages 5, 8 top and bottom and 9 bottom: Frank Spooner Pictures; page 6: Aladdin's Lamp; page 7: Eye Ubiquitous; pages 9 top, 12 through to 24: Sutton Photographic; page 11: Terence Cuneo painting by the kind permission of New Cavendish Books; page 24-25: British Film Institute.